DESIGN & TECHNOLOGY

IN PROCESS

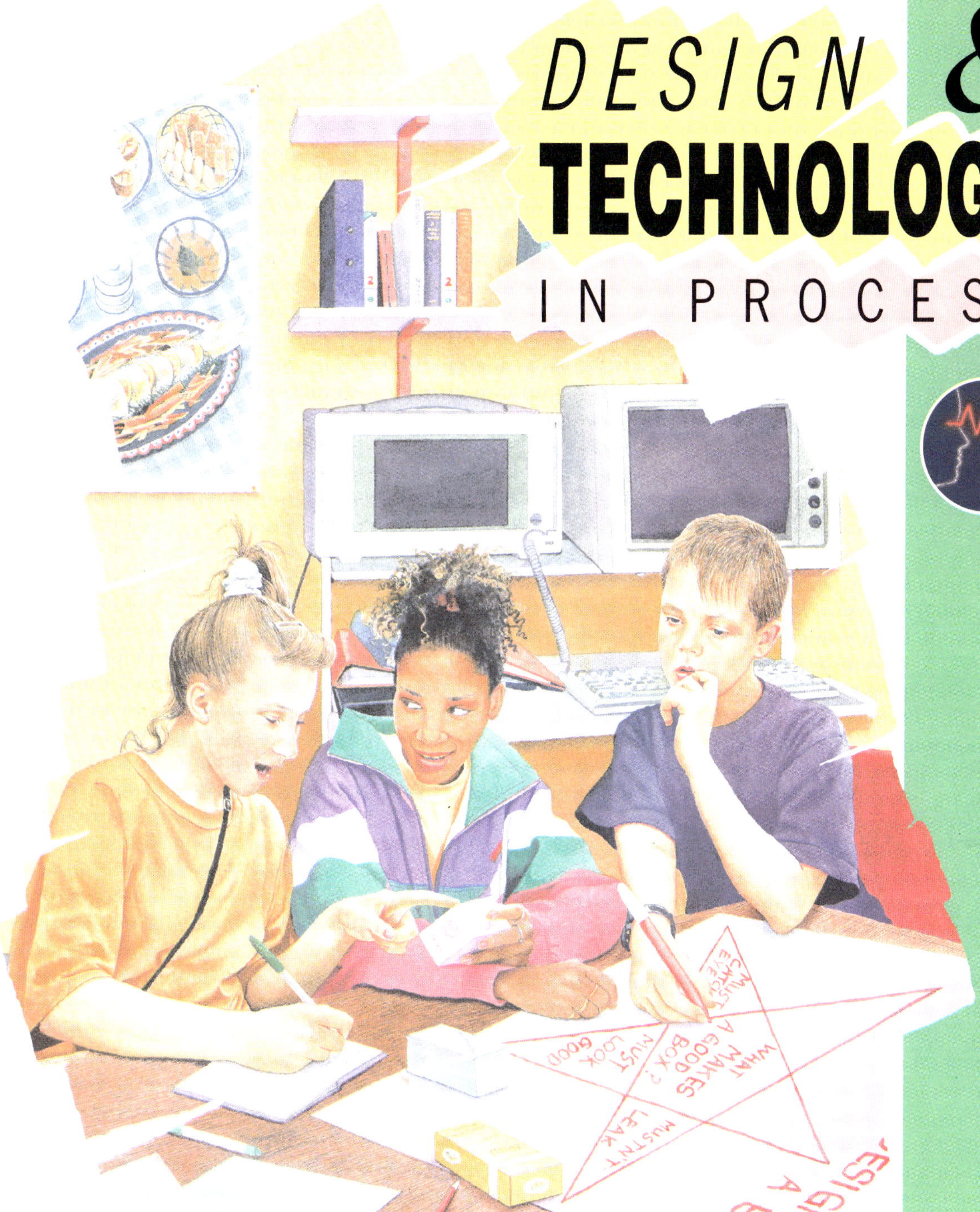

THE SKILLS BOOK

CONTENTS

Use this contents list to help you find the skills you need, when you need them.

THE SKILLS BOOK

Key

Introducing Design and Technology

Discuss, record and present

Research

Evaluate, test and record

Plan, design and make

WHAT IS DESIGN AND TECHNOLOGY?

Many of you will have experienced Design and Technology. You may have made puppets for a puppet show, a poster advertising a concert, or part of a meal for an end of term party.

Discuss

In your groups, explain to each other what experiences you have had of Design and Technology.

- What did you make?
- What tools and materials did you use?
- Did you work on your own or with others?

Record your group's ideas.

Using and developing skills

Coming up with ideas and turning them into products that work is part of the **process** of Design and Technology.

Record

The people in the pictures are all using Skills in Design and Technology. Match each picture with one of these skills:

Planning	Recording
Testing	Designing
Making	Evaluating
Discussing	Planning
Researching	Reviewing
Presenting	

Record your group's ideas.

A

C

D

Discuss

- Which skills did you use in your own Design and Technology activities? Record your ideas.
- What other skills do you think are important in Design and Technology?

Record

At the back of this book there is a list of the things you will be able to do as you become more skilled in Design and Technology. You can use this list to help you check on your progress in Design and Technology. Record which ones you can already do.

How Can You Use Design and Technology in Process?

These books give you an exciting way of doing Design and Technology. They are full of interesting activities and design tasks and are organised in a way that will help you develop your skills.

There are four books in the series – **The Skills Book** (this book) and three other **theme** books: **Health and Fitness, Entertainment** and **Survival**.

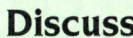

Discuss

In your group, look through one of the theme books.
- What skills are shown?

Now look at the contents list of this book. Find activities that develop these skills.

The Skills Book will help you with all the necessary skills you'll need to do your work. You can use it either *before* you start one of the tasks in one of the theme books or if you get stuck while you're working on a task.

Now look through the theme book. With your teacher, decide which theme tasks you'd like to tackle first.

Good luck! We hope you enjoy Design and Technology in Process.

PRODUCT TYPES

When something fits a purpose it is satisfying a need.
Products are designed to meet needs.

Discuss

The drawing of the snack biscuit shows some of the parts that have been designed.

Look at the parts which are labelled.

- What need does each part meet? If you need help look at **Information Sheet SB1**.

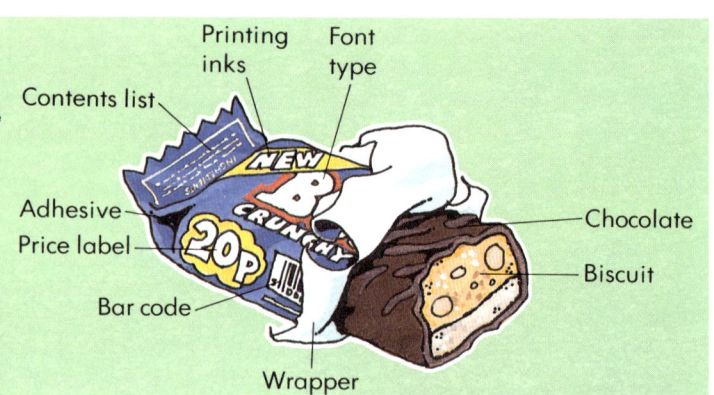

Printing inks · Font type · Contents list · Adhesive · Price label · Bar code · Wrapper · Chocolate · Biscuit

Artefacts, Systems and Environments

An object made by people is an **artefact** ▶ A set of objects or activities which perform a task is a **system** ▶ The surroundings made or developed by people is an **environment** ▶

Products can be put into three different groups. A product can be an **artefact**, a **system** or an **environment**.

Discuss

Look at the pictures of the three design products. ▼

SONY WALKMAN SYSTEM OR ARTEFACT?

In your group, decide which is an artefact, a system or environment.

Cut out the pictures on **Information Sheet SB2.**

Sort out the items into the three groups — artefact, system or environment.

- Are there any which fit into more than one group?

Discuss how *you* could **record** your sorting. The diagram may give you some ideas. ▲

Record

- Use the method you have chosen to record your sorted pictures. Stick the cut outs in place to make your record.

Research and Present

- Look through magazines, newspapers and catalogues. Choose and cut out different products and sort them into the three groups.
- Make a poster of product types.

Identifying Artefacts, Systems and Environments

When something is designed and made to fit a purpose it is satisfying a need. **Design meets a need.** But there are many different sorts of needs and many different types of products designed to meet them.

An artefact – an object made by people

A system – a set of objects or activities which perform a task

An environment – surroundings made or developed by people

SATISFYING A NEED

There are many different ways of satisfying a need. You can design a product in different materials, shapes, sizes and styles.

Look at the diagram and photographs and discuss them in your group.

Discuss and Record

- Which item do you think is likely to be picked by each person in the drawings.
- What are the reasons for your choice?

Discuss and Evaluate

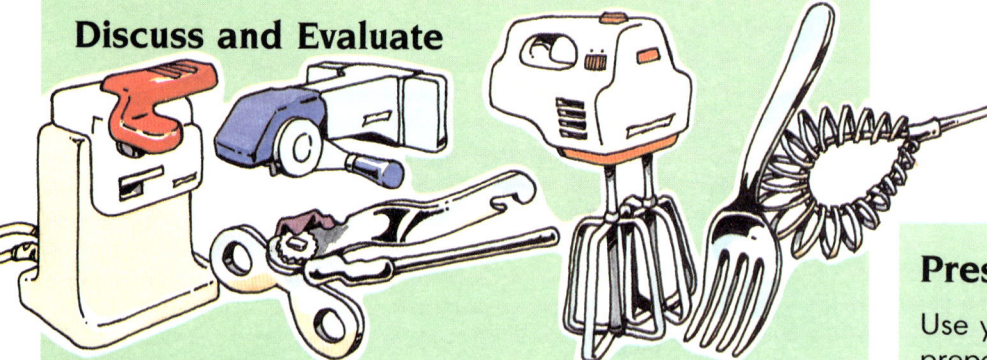

Collect one set of items from your teacher. Examine each one.

- Find out how each one works. If you can, take the item apart.
- Try using each one. Which one does the best job?
- Explain why you think the items are different prices. Remember, it may not *only* be the cost of materials.

Record your reasons.

If you were going on a camping trip, you might want to take one of these items.

- Which would you choose as the *one* item from the set to carry and use on a camping trip?

Record the reasons for your choice.

Present

Use your evaluation to prepare a report on the set of items to show others what you have found out.

- You could design and make a small advert for the items to compare the different features of each one.
- You could make a chart to show the results of your investigation, for a camping magazine.
- Can you think of another way to present your ideas?

Evaluate and Discuss

Sometimes a design changes as different materials become available or as people have better ideas or want things to look different.

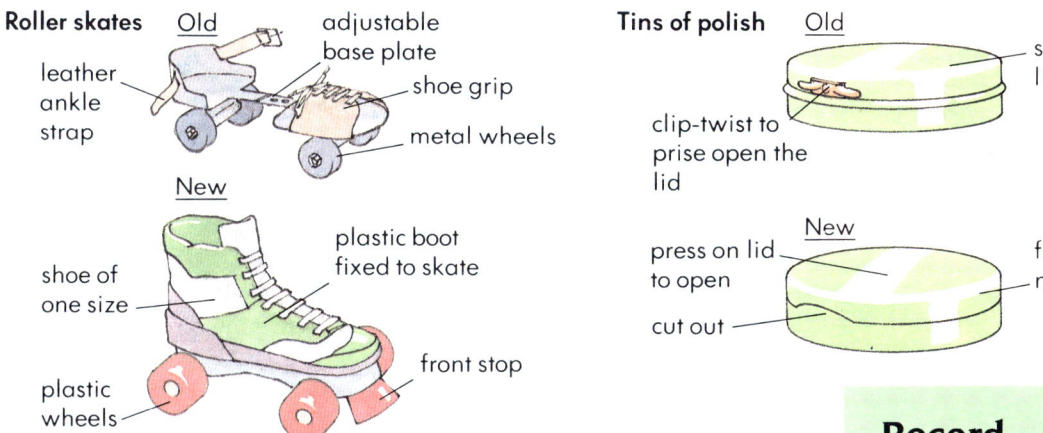

Roller skates Old
leather ankle strap
adjustable base plate
shoe grip
metal wheels

New
shoe of one size
plastic boot fixed to skate
plastic wheels
front stop

Tins of polish Old
stiff metal lid
clip-twist to prise open the lid

New
press on lid to open
cut out
flexible metal lid

Look at the diagrams and discuss them in your group.

- How has the design of each product changed?
- Why do you think the designs have changed? Could this be because of new materials? natural materials running out? someone inventing a new process? changes in fashion? any other reasons?

Meeting the Need

You often have a choice of items which will meet a need. The item you choose to use may depend on:

its purchase price,
the expense of using it,
the way it performs,
whether it's reliable,
the materials used in its manufacture,
its fashion appeal.

Technologists and designers consider these things whenever they design an **artefact, system,** or **environment**.

Designs may change as new materials are discovered or made and others begin to run out.

ELECTRICITY IS GOING UP AGAIN! IT'LL COST A LOT TO RUN

I WONDER WHAT THE SERVICE AND REPAIR COSTS ARE LIKE?

I CAN MAKE NICER GARMENTS WITH MY OLD KNITTING NEEDLES

I CAN'T AFFORD THAT! THERE'S A CHEAPER MODEL MADE BY KNITWELL

I HOPE THE FRAME ISN'T MADE OF TROPICAL HARDWOOD!

SPORTING CHANCE

By the 1960s cinder tracks were being replaced by synthetic materials. In 1964 the first resin 'Tartan' track was used at the Tokyo Olympics.

Roger Bannister's running shoes had soft leather uppers and a thin sole with metal spikes. Today a competitive runner wears shoes with plastic spikes and soles and uppers made from a mixture of natural and synthetic materials.

Discuss

- What sorts of things have caused changes in the designs of running shoes? Use the picture and information above to help you.

In Oxford in 1954 Roger Bannister made sporting history. He ran the first sub-four minute mile on a track made of cinders.

Discuss and Record

The people shown in the pictures all need something different from their special shoe. Discuss their needs.

Record your ideas

Collect **Information Sheet SB3.**

- Use your discussion to make changes to the statements on the sheet, if necessary.
- Cut out the boxes in the three columns.
- Match each person with their need and special shoe.

Record your matching by fixing the cut outs in your folder.

Research

The pictures above show how sports gear and equipment has changed since the early 1900s. Choose one sport. It may be one that is not shown in the photos. For the sport you choose use information books at school and in libraries to find out:

- what equipment is used and what needs it must meet.
- if, and how, the equipment has changed over the years.
- the way 'old' and 'new' designs and materials meet those needs.
- if these changes have helped to improve performance in the sport. Can you get details of records in your chosen sport over the years?

You could also ask sports people and sports manufacturers for information.

Remember to **record** all your information. Spread 0.13 will help you carry out your research.

Present

Decide how you are going to present your findings. You could make a poster, or write an article for the school or class newspaper, or make notes for your own use. Try to show all that you found out from your research.

- You could cut out pictures from sports magazines.
- You could include diagrams and charts.

GETTING IT ALL TOGETHER

A fastfood meal is prepared by a team of people. Each person in the team does a different job but they all work together to get the meal to the customer. Everyone in the team must know what they have to do.

HOW DO WE SORT OUT THE TASKS? WHO WILL DO WHAT?

Discuss and Plan

Use the recipes and preparation details on **Information Sheet SB4** to prepare a meal in 45 minutes.

Imagine you are organising three people to work in a group: Aisha, Billie and Chris.

In your group, discuss the recipes and the preparation shown on the sheet.

- Cut out each numbered step and give them to Aisha, Billie and Chris, so that the work is divided *fairly* between them.

Remember:
- each person must be working for some of the time.
- all parts of the meal must be ready in 45 minutes or less.
- the hot parts of the meal must be served hot.
- the table must be laid and the dishes washed.

When you have worked out the steps for each person stick them in the places on the **Information Sheet SB5.**

0.4

FIRST, WE HAVE TO WORK OUT HOW MUCH TIME EACH TASK WILL TAKE

HOW MANY PEOPLE NEED TO BE INVOLVED?

WE'LL HAVE TO GIVE EACH PERSON A TASK AND A TIME-LIMIT SO THAT EVERYTHING'S READY TOGETHER

Research and Discuss

Suppose your class is going on an outing at the end of the school day and no one has time to go home first to have a meal. Choose, plan, prepare and make a snack meal for your own group.

Before you choose the recipes you will need to find out the **constraints** — there will be some limits to what you can do:

- What cooking facilities are available?
- How much can each person pay?
- How much time do you have for preparation?

Record this information

Look at recipe books. Discuss the recipes you like.

- Which ones can you make within your constraints?
- Choose a meal which you can make with the time, money and equipment you have available.

Plan

Decide on the ingredients and the equipment you need. Discuss all the steps that have to be done to prepare the meal.

- How will you divide up the steps, fairly?

Plan how the work needs to be carried out.
- What is the sequence of the steps? You could use a flow diagram to work this out.

Record

Record your menu and your plan.

Show these to your teacher.

- If you can, prepare your meal . . . and enjoy it!

0.4

MONEY BOX

> We try to get children to save money and use banks by giving away money boxes . . . This helps them and us – wherever it goes the money box advertises the bank's name!

> These are O.K. but I'd like something in the box to move when I put my money in it.

Brainstorming Ideas

How would *you* set about designing an exciting '*Action*' money box for a young child?

In your group, each person works alone for five minutes.

- Think of things which happen around you.
- Think of things you thought were fun when you were young.
  The ideas in the drawings may help you. **0.6** may give you more ideas.
- How can you use your ideas for an '*Action*' money box?
- Record *all* your ideas – even the silly ones!

Discuss

Each person in the group explains one idea in turn.

One person writes down all the ideas on a large sheet of paper.

Keep going round the group until all the ideas are on the paper.

If you get a new idea as others read out theirs, note it down on your list and explain it when it is your next turn.

In your group look at and discuss the ideas.

- How are you going to make your choice?
- Choose the one you think will be most fun. You may decide to put two or more ideas together.

Present

Make a drawing of your money box design as you think it would look. Use **Information Sheet SB6** to help you.

You have made a **presentation drawing** of your design idea.

Thinking up design ideas like this is called Brainstorming.

Going Further

If you want to make your design, then you have a lot more work to do!

- Do you want to carry on working as a group or work on your own?

Discuss your ideas with your teacher. **0.6** may give you more ideas and help you make your 'action' money box.

Brainstorming

When you want to design something it's a good idea to start by **brainstorming** ideas. Sometimes you can get ideas from things around you.

When you brainstorm you:

- think of ideas linked to the need.
- share your ideas with others.
- choose ideas or parts of ideas that might work.
- work up your design idea into a drawing or description.

MOVING PARTS

Greeting cards and books sometimes have parts which you can move or which "pop-up" when you open the card or book.

Research

Look at a selection of cards and books which have moving parts.

You can examine ones that your teacher gives you or some that you may have at home.

- Open and close them so you can see how they "pop-up" or work in some way.
- Choose the one you like best.

Record

Describe how the card or book page you have chosen works.
- You could use diagrams and notes to explain this.

Show your description to others in your group.
- You may need to make some changes to make it clearer.

Making a model

Plan and Make

The diagrams show how to make different kinds of moving and pop-up cards.

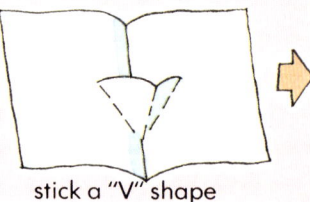

these first cuts could be a different shape . . .   or . . .   or . . .

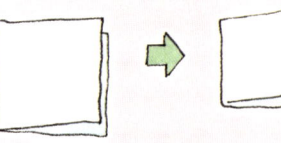

stick a "V" shape inside a card. Check the card closes and the shape pops open

fold in half, and in half again

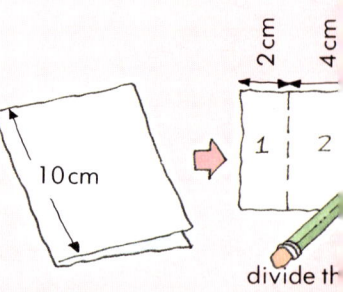

10cm   2cm   4cm   1   2

divide th[e] sections

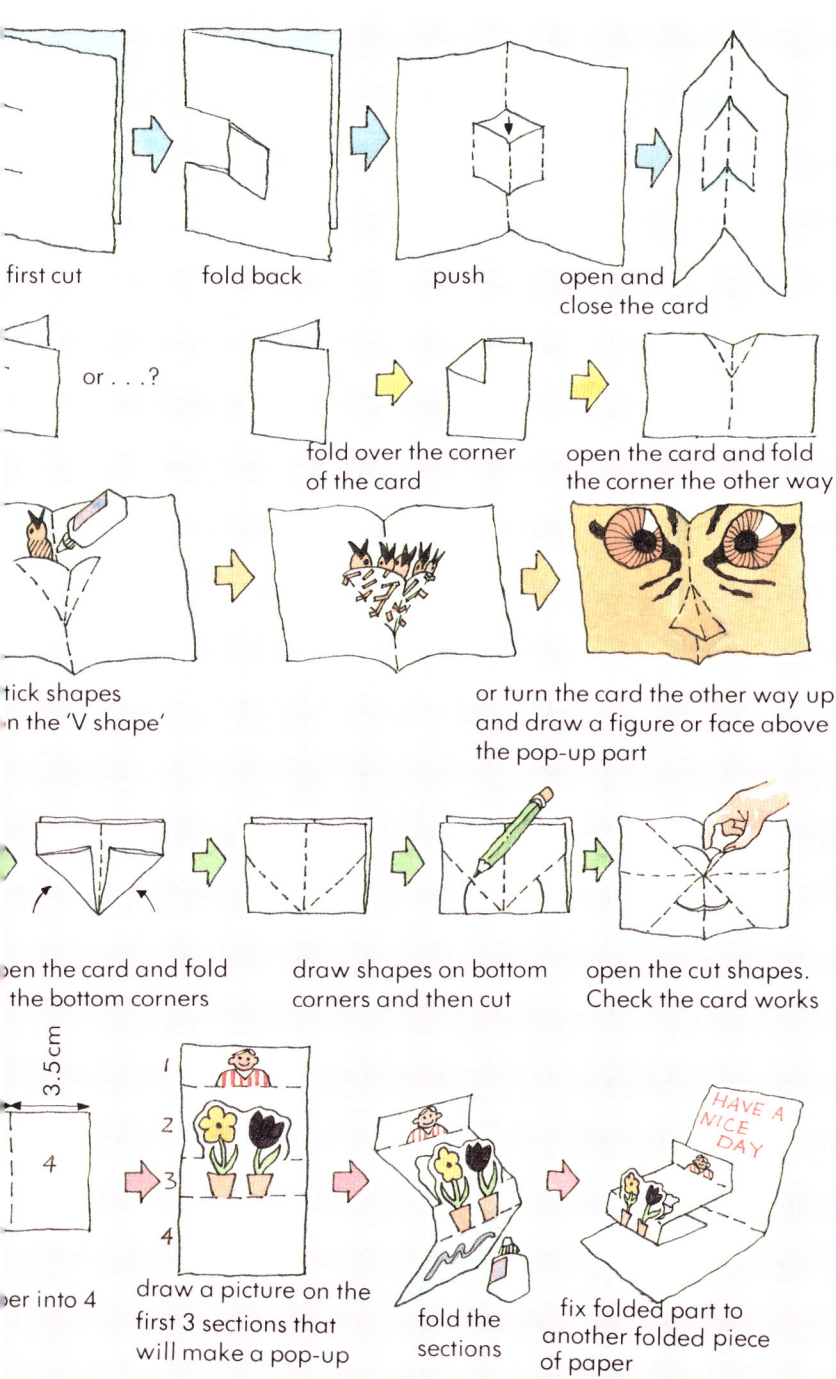

first cut   fold back   push   open and close the card

or . . .?   fold over the corner of the card   open the card and fold the corner the other way

tick shapes n the 'V shape'   or turn the card the other way up and draw a figure or face above the pop-up part

en the card and fold the bottom corners   draw shapes on bottom corners and then cut   open the cut shapes. Check the card works

er into 4   draw a picture on the first 3 sections that will make a pop-up   fold the sections   fix folded part to another folded piece of paper

se the diagrams to make these moving parts out of card.

What happens when you change things like the size of the parts or the position of any fold or cut? Try making these different changes.
What other changes could you make and try out?

ou have made a **model** to test a moving part. You have also sed the model to try out different ideas.

Record

Keep your models.

- If you found out something that was difficult to do or which needs to be done in a certain order, then record this.

Design and Make

Look at the cards and books again.

- **Brainstorm** some ideas for other moving card **mechanisms 0.5** will help you.
- Model one of these ideas.

Present

Explain to a friend or another group how your card works and how it was made.

- You could use diagrams and parts of the card to show how you made it.

PRESENTING THE CASE

Sometimes people set up pressure groups and organisations to try to draw attention to a problem that they think is important. They may decide to run a **campaign**, using leaflets, posters and events to pass on information and get attention for the cause.

You can organise a campaign about all sorts of things from a local issue to a world-wide problem.

Research and Discuss

Collect some examples of campaign items – posters, leaflets, tapes, videos and so on.

- You could write to pressure groups and organisations.
- Are there any local campaigns in your area? Try the library, town hall, hospital, community centre . . . or even your school!

In your group look at some of the items you have collected. Discuss and **record** the features of each item.

- How does it make its point? Is there a 'catch phrase'? Is the information easy to read? Is it eye-catching or funny?

Plan and Discuss

Plan a campaign about your chosen cause to convince others of your case. Use the ideas shown in the diagram to help you.

This could be folded into a pamphlet with an eyecatching image on the front.

You need to find evidence to support your case and decide how to spread this information

You could put the information on an information sheet. You should try to give answers to questions people might ask.

You may have to speak at a public meeting. You could use slides or overhead transparencies to illustrate your talk.

You must be ready to answer questions that the audience may ask . . . you may have to deal with some angry opponents.

You could make posters to display in public or carry on marches. You could use photographs on their own or as part of a poster or other document.

You could try to think of a fun event to publicize your cause.

In your group you will need to decide:

- what information you need to find out for your campaign.
- what items you want to make to present the information.
- how to divide up the tasks — who does the research? who designs the material? who thinks up the 'catch phrases'? Try to use the skills of the people in your group.
- what materials and equipment you need. How will you use the materials that are available?

Record

- Record your plan and your list of materials and equipment.

Show these to your teacher.

Make and Present

- Make, if you can, some or all of the items you have planned.
- Present your campaign to other members of your class.

Evaluate

Any campaign item should give information.

- How will you find out if each of the campaign items gave the information you wanted to others?
- What improvements could you make?

Designers often work on several projects at once. They have to keep all their work in order so that they don't lose any good ideas.

When you are designing you will produce lots of drawings and notes. You will need to keep your work in order too – and you'll need some sort of system in which to store your work.

Discuss

Brainstorm ideas for keeping your work in order.

- You could code each drawing or piece of information with a number and title according to the project, for example RB 1 (for your Rollaball work).
- You could date each piece and file your work in date order.
- Do you want to include your name or your group's name?
- What sort of abbreviations could you use?

Record your ideas.

Research and Discuss

Some schools may use ready-made files or folders for their design and technology work.

- What happens in your school?
- Look at other systems in stationery shops and catalogues.

In your group discuss:

- the way to store your work. Should you use a folder, a binder, a book . . . any other system?
- the size of the storage system?

- the kind of information you need at the front of the system so you can find things easily . . . a contents list? Could you divide it into sections for different projects?
- How will you keep your work clean and protected?

Design and Make

Use your research and discussion ideas to design and make your storage system.

- You could adapt your school folder.

Evaluate

Organise your storage system so you can use it for your projects.

- Can you store and find your work easily?
- Does your work stay clean and neat when it's in the system?
- Are there any changes you could make to improve your system?

FRONT COVER

The Design Brief

Jackie and Danny wrote this book. Together with Eluned, the editor, they told the designer what they wanted the front cover of the book to look like. They want the cover to show the right **product image**.

The front cover of the book is very important. It helps to show what the book is about and makes people notice it. I think we should get a graphic designer to do the design.

The designer needs to know what the book is about and what it should look like.

We need to write a brief for the designer which gives all the important information.

The Heinemann team prepared this design brief for Ron Kamen, the **graphic designer**. ▼

Design Brief: Skills Book Front Cover

- The cover should appeal to young people and teachers.
- Images should show: Technology, Design.
- The titles must be eye-catching and easy to read.
- The cover should have a logo that will identify all the books as part of a series.
- The logo should show that Design and Technology is about thinking and doing.

Developing Ideas

Ron used the brief to develop ideas for the cover. He looked for ideas from his previous work and from pictures in magazines and books. He then sketched some ideas and discussed these with the team.

These are some of the ideas Ron developed for the cover design. He tried out different ideas for the layout, the size and style of the type and for the logo.

Discuss and Evaluate

Look at the cover of this book.

- What changes did Ron make from his rough ideas to the final design?
- Did Ron satisfy the **criteria** in the design brief?

Could you use Ron's brief for a cover design for *your* 'designer storage' system on **0.8**?

- Which criteria would you leave out?
- Which new criteria would you include? What do you want your design to look like?

Record

List your design brief for the front cover of your storage system.

Remember it will need to have your name on.
- What other text will you need to include?

Design and Make

Use your design brief to design a cover for your storage system.

- Try different styles of writing.
- Try different styles of layout.
- You could design a logo for your class as part of the design

Decide the styles that you think are best and try to combine them in one sketch. Draw new sketches until you are happy with your design.

- Draw a full scale drawing of your best sketch.
- Keep a record of all your sketches in your folder.

Evaluate

Ask the others in your class to comment on your design.

- Check that it matches your design brief. You may want to make slight changes before you transfer your design to your storage system.

TOWER BRIDGE

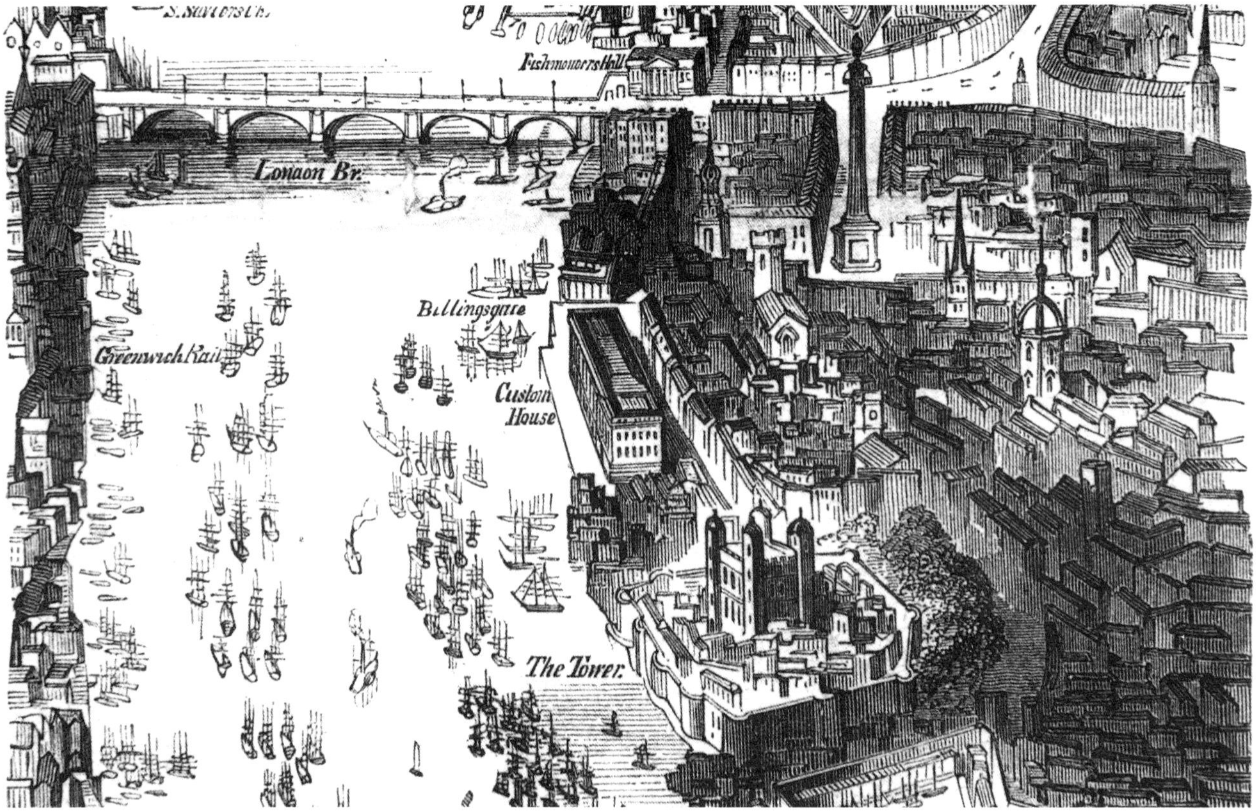

Over 100 years ago, when Victoria became queen, London was a growing city. More people were setting up businesses and bringing goods in and out. Traffic was increasing on the roads and on the River Thames. At that time, London was the busiest port in the world. The London docks were crowded and the river was full of shipping. People decided that a new bridge would help the traffic problems.

A committee was set up to look into the building of a new bridge to cross the river near the Tower of London. They asked architects and engineers to send in designs.

The committee thought up these conditions that the design needed to meet.

- The bridge had to allow tall masted ships to pass.
- The bridge must not need warehouses and wharves to be knocked down. It had to be built keeping buildings and surroundings intact.
- The bridge must not have long steep approach roads.

Conditions like these are called the **criteria** for a design.

Here are four designs that the committee received.

1

2

Discuss and Record

Bridge **4** was the design that the committee picked.

- Discuss how each of the other three designs did not meet the criteria.

Record your ideas.

> The actual Tower Bridge is a revised version of Bridge 4. Can you spot the differences?

Discuss

The committee chose design number **4** because it matched the criteria better than the others.

- How do you think the successful bridge matched the criteria?
- How do you think the new bridge *did* affect the lives and the **environment** of people in London?

Present

You could make up a short story or play about the building of Tower bridge. Use the ideas from your discussion above.

> When you decide the conditions that a design should meet you are setting the *criteria* for the design.

4

LIFEBOAT

In the 1850s thousands of people lost their lives at sea. Many ships were wrecked near to the shore because they were forced against rocks during storms. At that time ships did not have lifeboats.

More than 100 years ago, the Royal National Lifeboat Institution (RNLI) was set up. It organised a competition to design a lifeboat. The Institution listed the **criteria** for the design of the boat. You can find out more about setting criteria on **0.10**.

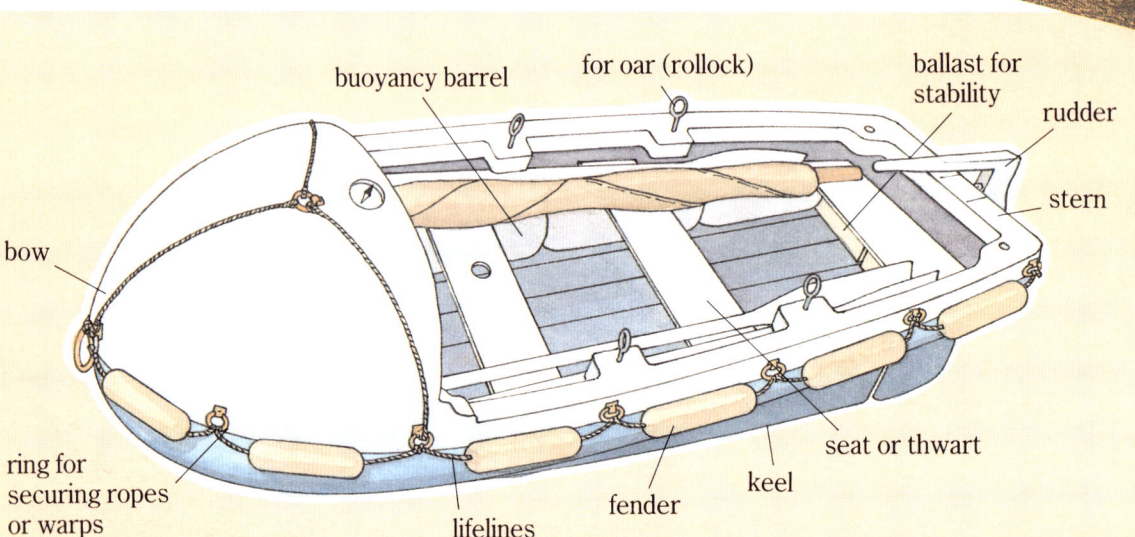

The design for the lifeboat must have the following qualities:

Serve as a rowing boat in all weather	20
Serve as a sailing boat in all weather	18
Serve as a sea boat; be stable, safe, be able to launch forward through surf	10
Have an internal capacity of water up to level of thwarts	9
Have a means of freeing water	8
Have extra buoyancy	7
Have self-righting power	6
Have space and power for accommodating passengers	3
Have weight for transportation	3
Have protection of boats bottom	3
Have ballasting	3
Have stem and stern access	3
Have timber head for securing warps	2
Have fenders, lifelines	1
	100

Each criterion was given a score. Why do you think the RNLI did this?

Look at the competition document. The drawing above may help you understand the words.

The list contains all the criteria. It shows what the RNLI wanted in a lifeboat design. This document is called the **design brief**. Each competitor was given this design brief to follow.

Design and Record

Look at the list of criteria and decide why you think each one is important.

Record your decisions

Pick out the criteria that would mean the boat could:

- get to a shipwreck,
- cope with stormy weather,
- stay afloat even when full of water,
- carry people.

Record the reasons for your answers.

Discuss

Over 280 entries were received in the lifeboat competition. Each included a scale model of the design and working drawings and estimates of the cost. The best fifty were displayed at the Great Exhibition of 1851. The winner was James Beaching, he scored 84 out of a possible 100 points.

- No one scored 100 points in the competition. Why do think this was so?

Discuss and Record

Modern lifeboats can save lives far out to sea in conditions that would have wrecked Beaching's boat.

- If a competition for a lifeboat was being organised now, what other criteria do you think would be listed?

A design brief is a clear statement of what is needed in a design.

Stating a Design Brief

A design brief is a clear statement of what is needed. A manufacturer or client writes the design brief for the designer or technologist, who use it to design and make the product. Sometimes you cannot match all the criteria but technologists and designers try to meet the most important ones. For example the design brief for this kettle would state that it must:

- Be made of materials that can hold boiling water.
- Be easy to pick up and pour.
- Be safe to use – all electric parts must be insulated.
- Have a lid that comes on and off easily.
- Look stylish and modern.

Can you think of any other criteria that the design brief might list?

SMELL OF SUCCESS

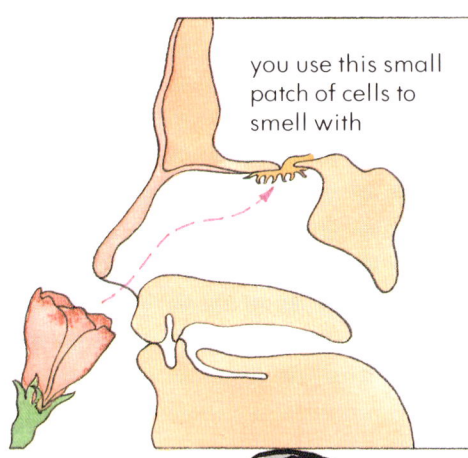

you use this small patch of cells to smell with

Did you know your sense of smell is a stamp size patch of cells inside your nose?

Did you know most animals have a better sense of smell than us and they used it to find food, follow a trail or find a mate.

Did you know doctors used to diagnose disease by smelling the patient's breath? Typhoid smells of baking bread.

FISH 'N' CHIPS

Did you know there are over 6000 chemicals with a smell? People describe them by linking the smell with something. You can say something smells "strong", "hot", "damp" or "floral".

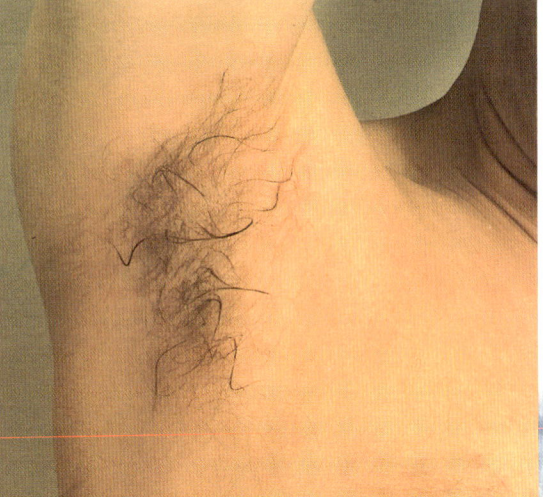

Your most powerful body smells are made by glands in your armpit. When you sweat during exercise or when you are excited or frightened glands give off these smells. Fragrance manufacturers try to find smells you like and disguise the ones you don't!

Smells annoy people. Manufacturers make products to disguise smells . . . they also make bad smells too!

Preference sampling

When you want to find out what people like or dislike, you cannot ask everyone, so you just ask some. This is called taking a **sample**. When you ask a sample to find out what they *prefer* you are doing a **preference sampling** survey using a **testing panel**. Manufacturers use their research from preference sampling to design new products.

Using a testing panel to find the best smell for a soap powder.

Discuss

In your group, you will try to find out which smells people like or dislike. You will be able to use this information in the design of a new smell. You need to decide:

- how many people will be in your sample,
- if you will use people of a certain age range, like 10–12 year olds, or people from one or both sexes. This will be your **target group**.
- the smells you are going to use,
- the way you are going to get people to sniff the smells.
- how to make your testing fair.
- how you are going to record what you find out.

Information Sheet SB7 may give you some ideas.

Present

Carry out your preference sampling survey. Write a report of your results. Remember to:

- describe how you organised the sample and were fair,
- present a table of your findings,
- summarise your findings so it is clear which smells people like or dislike.

You can use your work on preference sampling to design a new smell on **0.19**.

When you test a sample of people to find out their preferences you are carrying out a preference sampling survey.

FINDING OUT

Researching Information

When you are designing something you often need to **research** your ideas.

There are many ways you can find out information. When you are **researching** a topic you need to decide what sort of information you're looking for and where to find it. . . .

Recording Information

Whenever you look for information, you need to keep a record of *what you find out* and *where* you found it. You could keep your records in a folder. The diagram shows one way you could keep your records.

Information	Source	Number of sheet in folder
Names and phone nos + addresses of music shops	Yellow pages	1.
Photos of instruments	Own photographs, copies of pictures from books and magazines.	In envelope ② In envelope ③

Discuss

You are going to find out how to use the different sources of information shown in the diagram above.

Decide on the topic you want to research. You could research a topic for an activity in Design and Technology or in another subject.

You could find out about:

- Children's book covers on "eggs and hens", "fishes", "trees," "elephants". . . .
- Spelling games for children.
- Bags for sports equipment.
- Personal stereos.
- The programme for an event.

The topic you are researching may have information about it under another heading or title. So before you start, **brainstorm** the topic in your group so you can come up with all the possible links.

You could record your ideas in a diagram.

Research

Once you have picked your topic and worked out the other headings and lists connected to it, share out all the possible sources of information amongst your group. Use all the sources to research the topic.

- Each person may have to research more than one source. (Someone could research books and magazines).
- Remember to keep a research file and to list all the information you collect.

Discuss and Evaluate

In your group, discuss how useful you found each type of source.

Tell each other about such things as:

- how easy it was for you to understand the information you found.

- if the information you found was up to date.
- if pictures were available.
- if the information gave you hints about other places to look.
- whether it cost anything to get the information.

Evaluate

- How will you decide which was the most useful source?
- What difference does the type of topic make as to how useful a source is or isn't?
- How do you decide what *is* or *is not* useful information?

Present

Prepare a report on the topic you have researched.

- Remember to describe how you found out the information and which was the most useful source.
- Include the difficulties your group came across when they were researching. Can you think of ways of getting round these?

0.13

QUESTIONS, QUESTIONS

40% of holiday makers in Scotland go to see the scenery!

59% of children notice firework warnings on schools posters

Nearly half the adult population listen to Radio 1

The average number of radios in each home is 3.76

Did you know. . . . ?

Questions, questions . . .

WHICH SOFT DRINK FLAVOUR DO 13 YR. OLDS LIKE BEST ?

WHAT PRICE WILL PEOPLE PAY FOR A NEW TYPE OF BISCUIT ?

WHY IS "NEIGHBOURS" SO POPULAR?

HOW FAR WILL PEOPLE TRAVEL TO WATCH AN ATHLETICS MATCH ?

WHAT IS THE TOP SELLING ALBUM THIS WEEK ?

Market researchers find out information and the answers to questions like these. They often use questionnaires to collect opinions and information.

Questions . . .

Discuss and Evaluate

Look at the question pairs on **Information Sheet SB8**.

Discuss each pair of questions.

Decide which one in each pair would be the most helpful if you were trying to find out how people use anti-perspirants. Think about:

- what sort of information the answer will give.
- how easy the question is to answer.

Look at the 'Numbers' section on **Information Sheet SB8**. Ten people were asked question **A** and **B**.

- Which question gave the most useful information?

Record

Use your evaluation to make a list of what makes a good question.

For example:

- a good question does not ask people to remember unusual facts.
- a good question does not use technical words.

This list is your **criteria** for *a good question.*

. . . and Questionnaires

HOW DO YOU DESIGN A QUESTIONNAIRE ?

YOU NEED TO DECIDE WHAT **TYPES** OF QUESTIONS WILL WORK WELL.. HOW YOU SHOULD WORD THEM..HOW YOU SHOULD ORDER THEM..

.. YES, AND THIS LIST OF KEYPOINTS ARE YOUR **CRITERIA** FOR DESIGNING A GOOD QUESTION-NAIRE

SO I NEED TO DECIDE THESE THINGS FIRST & RECORD THEM..

Discuss and Evaluate

Look at the questionnaire on **Information Sheet SB9**. If possible try to do this questionnaire.

Use this questionnaire to list what makes a good questionnaire.

- Look at each question. If necessary, add to your criteria for what makes a good question.
- Look at the complete questionnaire. How is it structured? Can you fill it in quickly?

Record your **criteria** for what makes a *good questionnaire*.

"KAYNINE TASTY CHUNKS" AREN'T SELLING WELL. I NEED TO KNOW WHICH DOG-FOOD MOST PEOPLE BUY AND WHY THEY BUY IT. THEN I MIGHT BE ABLE TO CHANGE KAYNINE'S IMAGE.

KAYNINE PRODUCTS

Design and Make

Design and make a questionnaire to find out about something that interests you. You could find out:

- which is the most popular kind of holiday and what are the reasons for its popularity.
- which is the most popular personal stereo and how could it be improved.
- which kind of wall coverings and displays do people want on their bedroom walls.

- something else you would like to know about the people in your class or school.

Decide on the information you need to collect.

Design some questions and build them up into a questionnaire.

- Decide on your sample size. Look at **0.12** for more help on samples.

Evaluate

Try out your questionnaire on a few people.

- Is it giving you the information you want. Do you want to make any changes?

Use your questionnaire on a chosen sample. Analyse their answers.

Present

Present your findings to the class. Try to:

- show what your survey was about,
- tell them what you discovered or found out,
- include the questionnaire,
- describe how you used the questionnaire,
- give details of your sample, – how many? what age? etc.
- You could present your findings as a bar chart, table or in some other way.

0.14

WHAT'S IN AN AD?

People advertise all sorts of things in newspapers.

Any advert is designed to make you *do* something – buy, visit, donate and so on.

Discuss and Evaluate

GREAT OFFER

60 capsules Evening Primrose Oil 250 mg for JUST £1.00 **(NORMALLY £3.35)** Send £1.00 NOW to **BIO NUTRITION LTD, PO Box 18, Heathfield, East Sussex TN21 8BR.** quoting your Access/ Visa No or telephone us on 04352 5959

Plus you will receive our latest catalogue entitling you to a £5 discount voucher.

FILM PRODUCTION COURSE
at the National Film Theatre
(evenings) £135; a few places left.
Starts Tuesday 3 April
8 sessions
Ring 938 2222 ex. 2180
STREETLIGHT FILM PRODUCTIONS LTD

Wates
LETTING SERVICES

SW7 1 bedroom Apartment in newly refurbished development f/f from £170 pw excl.

SW3 2 bed –2 bath f/f flat, convenient location. Available now. £220 pw excl.

SE16 2 bedroom purpose built flat in new development. F/F. Underground, parking. £150 pw excl.

081–668 7161

Kurdish Cultural Centre – London 1990

NAWROZ FESTIVAL

TICKETS AVAILABLE ON DOOR

30th March 1990
Great Hall
Westminster Central Hall
Storey's Gate, London SW1

Time: Festival starts 2pm
Main event 4pm

Tickets: £12 waged
£8 unwaged
Available at:
KCC
14 Stannary St
London SE11 4AA
Tel: (071) 824 0861

Songs
Music and Dance
Exhibition
Play
Food

Organised by:
The Kurdish
Cultural Centre

In your group discuss what you think makes a good newspaper advert. These examples may give you some ideas.

- You could evaluate other adverts you've seen that are good.

Use the diagram below to help you. It shows you what each part of an advert does and what it is called. You may want to use these words when you record your ideas.

Record your ideas on what makes a good advert. These are your **criteria**.

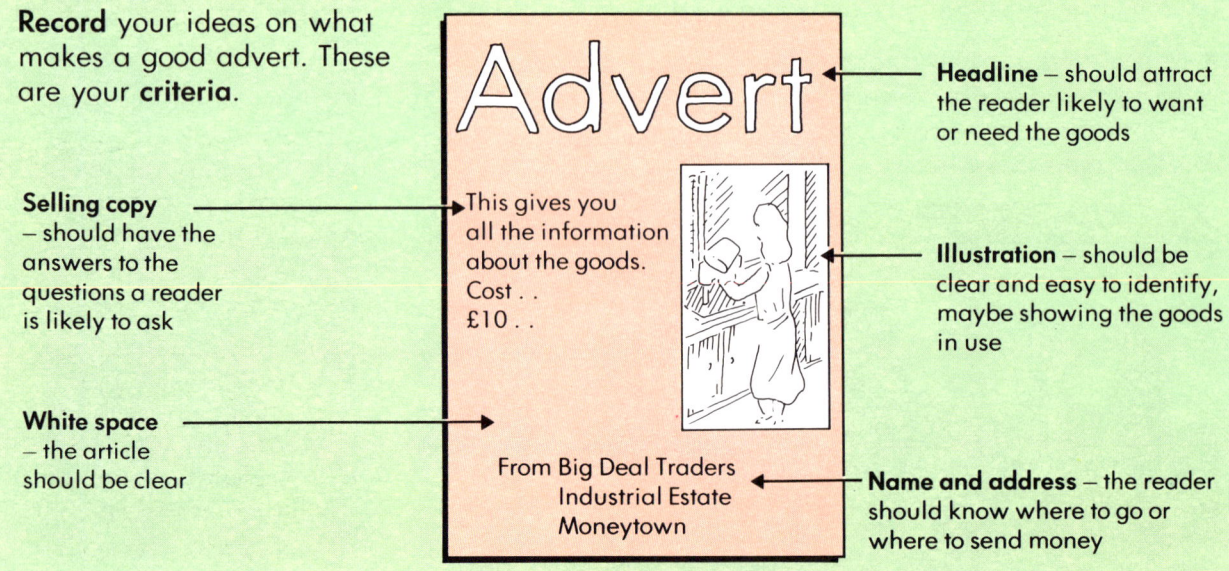

Selling copy – should have the answers to the questions a reader is likely to ask

White space – the article should be clear

Advert

This gives you all the information about the goods. Cost . . £10 . .

From Big Deal Traders Industrial Estate Moneytown

Headline – should attract the reader likely to want or need the goods

Illustration – should be clear and easy to identify, maybe showing the goods in use

Name and address – the reader should know where to go or where to send money

Evaluate and Record

Look through the advert pages in newspapers.

Cut out adverts which use the ideas on your list. You can also use the ones on **Information Sheet SB10**.

For each one decide:

- what the advert is trying to get you to do?
- who will the advert appeal to? – young people? women? gardeners?

These are fonts	This is style	This is size
Avant Garde	Demi	10 point
Times	*Italic Outline*	*18 point*
Helvetica	Narrow	24 point
New Baskerville	Bold	14 point
Garamond	*Bold Italic*	*12 point*
Souvenier	Light Italic	9 point
Futura	Heavy	8 point
Bodoni	**Poster**	**15 point**
Stone sans	Shadow	13 point

In your group, discuss how the designers use different type sizes, fonts and drawings to make an advert meet its purpose.

Record your decisions.

Design and Make

Sometimes schools and youth clubs advertise their events in newspapers.

- Use your criteria for a good advert to design and make a newspaper advert for an event. It could be a disco, a sporting event or the school play.
- Use the adverts shown here and on **Information Sheet SB10** to give you some ideas.

Present and Review

Present your ideas to others in your class.

- Explain what you think makes a good advert.
- Give examples of adverts that show the way designers use different type faces and drawings.
- Give examples of adverts your group think are good.
- Do other groups agree with you?
- Use their comments to make any changes to your list of criteria for a good advert.

Present and Evaluate

Present your advert to others in your class.
- Show how your advert matches your criteria.

Other students may have some different criteria for evaluating an advert.

- You could ask others to use their criteria to evaluate your advert.

ROLL A BALL

David wanted to make a puzzle for his brother. He found instructions in a book. These are shown on the **Information Sheet SB11**.

Make

Collect the tools and materials you need. These are given on **Information Sheet SB11**.

Follow the plan and make the puzzle.

Discuss and Evaluate

Jasia saw the puzzle David was making. She decided to make one for her friend Petra.

The diagram shows Jasia's design. She decided to use plywood for the base and square section wood for the uprights.

Look at the cardboard puzzle you have made.

- How does Jasia's design differ from your cardboard puzzle?

Record as many differences as you can.

- Which design do you think would last the longest?
- Which one do you think would be the cheapest to make?

200 mm
200 mm
10 mm
3 marbles
15 mm diameter
hollow to fit marble
plywood base
square section wood

Discuss

Use Jasia's design and the ideas in the photos to **brainstorm** ideas for your own puzzle design.

- It could be a different *shape*, or *size* or it could be made from different materials.
- What materials and equipment have you got available?

Make rough sketches of your ideas.

Design

Choose your best idea and **develop** drawings to show how to make it.

- You may want to make several drawings to show different parts of your design.

Your drawings should show:

- the sizes of the parts of your puzzle,
- the way to join the parts together.
- how the puzzle would be put together.
- any finishing patterns or colours.

Plan

Prepare a set of instructions for the making of your puzzle.
Look at **Information Sheet SB11** if you need help.

Your instructions should include:

- a list of the materials you need and *how much* you need.
- a description of how to cut the pieces to the right sizes.
- instructions on how to join the parts together.
- a list of the tools and equipment you need to use and notes on how to use them.

Discuss your ideas for cutting and joining the materials with your teacher:

- You may need to add some changes to your plan.
- If necessary, practice how to use some of the cutting and joining tools safely. Use **offcuts** of materials to practice on.

Make

- Collect the materials and tools you need from your teacher.
- Make your puzzle.

Record any changes you make to your design as you make your puzzle.

DESIGNER BOXES

A design consultant can provide help and design skills to all sorts of companies and manufacturers. You can use a design consultant to design anything from a whole new company image to a box for your new line in chocolates. . .

Once we know what the customer needs we then brainstorm as many ideas as possible.

Companies can come to us when they want new boxes designed for their products. These companies are called our clients.

We draw and discuss our ideas. This helps us to develop and improve the ideas as a team.

*Once we've come up with an idea we like. I draw how I think the box will actually look. This is called a **presentation drawing**.*

*I make drawings to show clearly how the box should be made. These are called **working drawings**.*

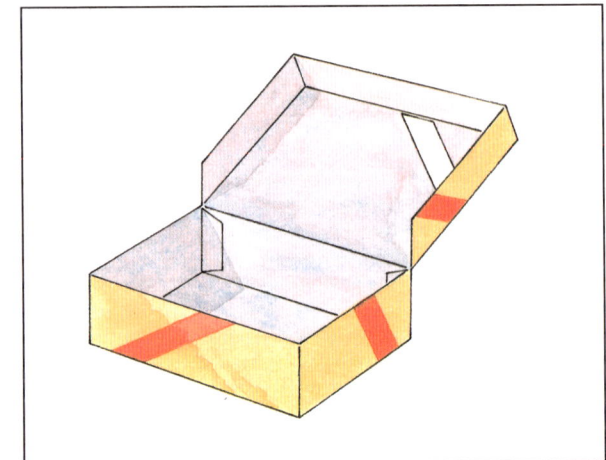

We use the presentation drawings and working drawings to show what the box will look like and how it will be made.

The drawings also help us to calculate the amount and cost of materials and labour.

It also helps to sell our design to the customer if we can show them a model of the box. Also when we make the model we may find faults in the design then we change the design to solve these.

We can use these drawings to show the customer our ideas . . and make any changes if necessary.

Discuss and Record

You are going to design and make a box for an item.

- Decide on the item – it should be something you can get hold of easily.
- **Brainstorm** your ideas for the kind of box you would like to make. The photos shown here may give you some ideas.
- Make rough sketches of your ideas.

Design and Make

Choose your best idea and do a **presentation drawing** to show what your box will look like.

Make **working drawings** to help you plan the making of your box. Remember you will have to think about:

- the size of the box. How will the item fit in?
- whether the box will have a separate lid.
- how it is to be cut from a sheet of card.
- whether it will have overlapping edges to allow gluing.
- whether you will decorate the box while it is a flat sheet.

Plan and Review

List the materials and equipment you will need to make your box.

Discuss your drawings and plans with your teacher. Use them to make a model of your box.

- What materials are you going to use to make your model? Remember you want it to look as realistic as possible.
- Are there any changes you could make to improve your design?

If possible, make your final design.

Drawings and models help to develop a design from an idea to a final product.

MODELLING YOUR HOME

Architects like Ann Sawyer work closely with the people who are going to live in the buildings she designs. She tries to make sure the designs meet their needs. Before she starts work on a design she finds out what the residents would like – this is part of her **design brief**. As she works she does drawings and models to develop her ideas. . .

'I'm a community architect. I designed these flats working with the people who live in them.'

Ann produces many working drawings to show ▲ exactly how everything in the building fits together. The builders follow these plans closely.

Ann produces presentation drawings and models to ▲ show people what the building will look like – inside and outside.

Ann designs the lay-out of each flat in the block. She has to decide where all the doors and windows, furniture and fittings will go. She uses **scale drawings** and model furniture to test her ideas. She uses these models and drawings to **brainstorm** her ideas with the residents. ▼

Discuss and Record

You are going to design the lay-out of a room 4 m × 2.5 m. Decide on the type of room you would like to design and model.

- You could model a bedroom, kitchen, living room . . any other room?
- What type of furniture and fittings will you want and how much?
- What size will the furniture need to be?
- Where should the doors and windows go?

Record your ideas with rough sketches – you may want to rough out many different ideas for laying out the room.

Plan and Make

Will your ideas work? You can test them.

Make a simple scale drawing of the room on squared paper.

- You may want to make your scale quite large so you have room for your models. If you use 10 mm square paper and allow 10 squares for 1000 mm (1 metre) this gives you a scale drawing of 1/10. This 1/10 scale will fit on an A3 sheet of paper.
- Mark out where the door and windows are going. Remember to draw them to scale. Make some measurements of real doors and windows in your home to give you some idea.

Plan how you could make model furniture and fittings for your room. You'll need to consider, size, colour and material.

Make a list of the tools and materials you need. Show these to your teacher and then make your models.

- Remember you need to be able to move your models around to test out different arrangements. You could use card, Lego, Duplo . . anything else?
- You need to make your models *to the same scale* as the room. You could make some measurements of furniture and fittings at home to give you an idea of their sizes.

Make a list of the tools and materials you need. Show these to your teacher and then make your models.

Design and Review

Use your scale drawing, models and rough ideas to design the lay-out of your room.

- **Information Sheet SB12** will help you think about some of the **constraints**.
- Test your ideas by moving the models into different arrangements. Ask other people in your group for their suggestions.
- What materials could you use to show what the floor and wall coverings will look like?
- Did you have to reject or change some of your original ideas? If so why, and how?

Present and Evaluate

Show your final design to others.

- You could do a **presentation drawing** of the finished lay-out.
- You could also make a 3D presentation model of your room design.
- Describe the colour scheme you have chosen and the reasons for your choice.
- Did your model help others to see what the room would look like?
- How did your model help you decide on what furniture and fittings you could fit in and how they could be arranged?

ODOUR BY ORDER

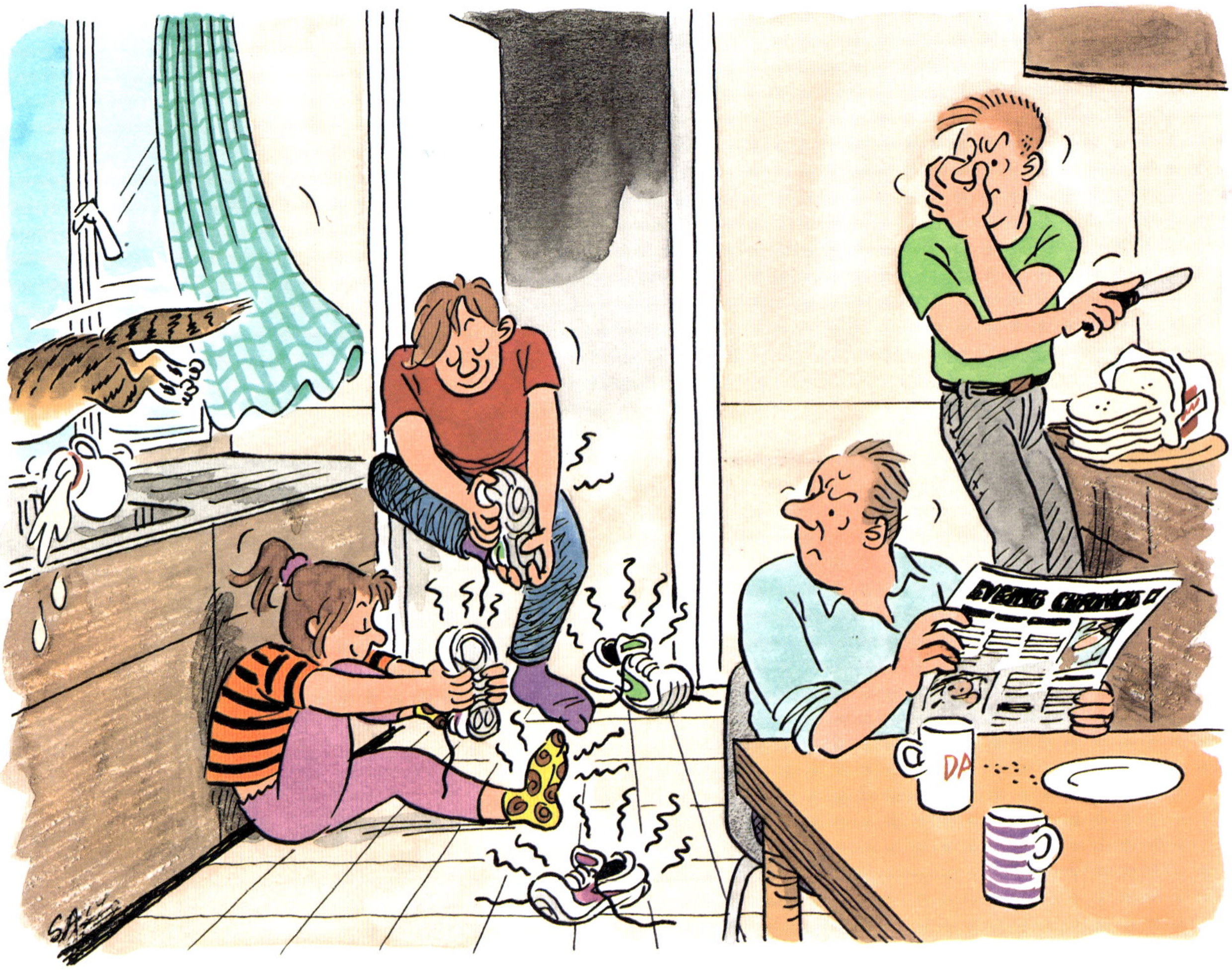

Feet sweat! . . . shoes and trainers start to smell! What can you do?

You can buy carbon pads to put inside your shoes. The carbon absorbs the smell.

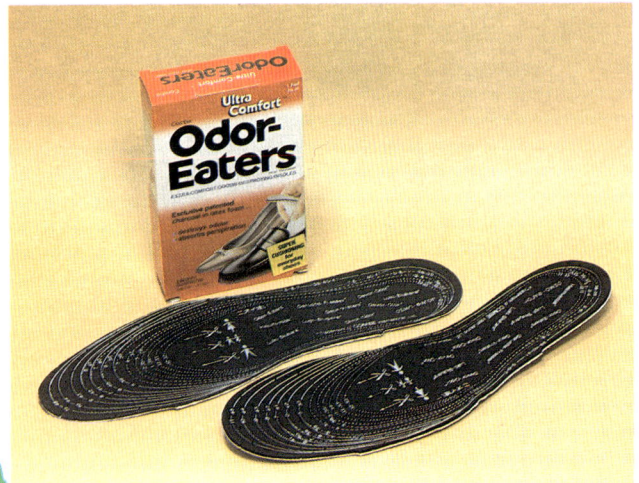

Supposing you want to design a new solution to the problem of smelly shoes! You want to make something that can be used on *any* shoe at *any* time. You could make a shoe spray but you need to find the right smell.

Discuss and Record

- Since the spray is to be used to freshen shoes what sort of smell should it have? **Brainstorm** some types of smell for the spray.
- Who do you most want the shoe spray to appeal to? Who is your **target group**?

Record your ideas.

Plan and Test

Smell of Success 0.12 is about the smells people like or dislike. You could use the information from this spread to work out how to make a new smell to satisfy the smelly shoes' need – then find out how your **target group** like it.

In your group decide what ingredients you are going to use to make the smell. It will be easier if you just use different combinations of *two* ingredients.

- Decide how you are going to combine the smells and record the combinations. The diagram may give you some ideas. ▼

Liquid smell A		Number of drops used				*These are variable*
Liquid smell B		0	1	2	3	
Number of drops used	0	0 0	1 0	2 0	3 0	
	1	0 1	1 1	2 1	3 1	
	2	0 2	1 2	2 2	3 2	
	3	0 3	1 3	2 3	3 3	
	4	0 4	1 4	2 4	3 4	

- Decide how you are going to test people and record your results. Remember, you need to find out which smell people like best.

The table below may give you some ideas on how to score the preferences of your target group. ▼

Remember you need to:

- try different combinations of smells
- record the combinations.
- test a sample of people in the target group in a fair way.
- record your findings.

	Number of drops		Least liked	Score			→
	A	B	1	2	3	4	5
Sample 1	3	0					
Sample 2	1	1					
Sample 3	2	1					

Present

Write a report of how you carried out your design and testing.

- Describe how you changed the ingredients in the smell.
- Show how you recorded the combinations.
- Summarise your findings so it is clear which combination is the most popular with your target group. You could use a block graph.
- Do you think other target groups would give the same results? How would you find out?

You have designed a component of a product. You have tested a sample of a target group to find out which smell is liked best.

SKILLS IN DESIGN AND TECHNOLOGY

As you progress through Design and Techonology in Process you will become more **capable** technologists. Here is a list of things you will be able to do as a capable technologist. At times during your course you will be asked to show that you can do these things.

Identifying Needs and Opportunities

3a I can use what I already know, and what I have found out from my investigations to decide on my Design & Technology activity.

3b I can talk about my ideas with people who know something about the activity to make sure my ideas make sense.

4a I can think of ideas for Design & Technology activities when I start work on a topic I have not looked at before.

4b I can use a variety of ways of getting information.

4c I can take into account the views of other people.

4d I know that I will not always be able to produce exactly what I want to because of lack of money, materials, equipment, time and skill, and that I have to make choices about what I can actually produce.

4e I can talk about and write about what I have found out from an investigation.

4f I know how people throughout history and in other countries have used Design & Technology to solve problems.

5a I can choose the best sources of information to use when searching for needs and opportunities for a Design & Technology activity.

5b I understand about economic, social, environmental and technological considerations and the effects these have on the people who use them.

6a I can explain clearly how I identified the needs and opportunities for a Design & Technology activity, and can give reasons for my decisions.

6b I can explain how different cultures have influenced design and technology.

6c I understand how new technologies offer new opportunities and create new demands for Design & Technology activities.

7a I can make use of information of several kinds, and am able to decide how to deal with conflicting ideas.

7b I can use a variety of methods in order to obtain all the information required.

7c I consider both the user and the producer.

7d I can make use of a range of expert advice as appropriate.

Generating a design

3a I can think up lots of ways of solving the problem, and can write about them, draw them and talk about them.

3b I can look at all my ideas and choose the one I think is best, explaining why I didn't choose the others.

3c I can use books, magazines and other information to help me find out if people in other countries or people in history have tried out ideas like mine.

3d I can make drawings and models to show how I think my idea will work.

3e I can look at different types of material such as card, plastic, cloth, wood and choose the sort of material that I think would work best for my idea.

4a I can write down and draw about how my ideas change as I am working.

4b I keep looking at my idea and try to find out ways of improving it.

4c I can work out the things I need for my task, and can check that all the things I need are available.

4d I can use a series of pictures (storyboard) to help me plan an activity.

5a I can show in detail how my ideas developed, and explain reasons for any changes.

5b I can take parts out of a number of different ideas and combine them into my new idea, explaining why I didn't use some of them.

5c I can find information from magazines, encyclopaedias, databases, videos and other people that will help me with my ideas.

5d I can check that the equipment and materials I need for my project are available, and if something is missing, I can change my design to take that into account.

5e I can plan out my project on paper using charts or flow diagrams.

6 I can choose the important features of a particular project.

7a I can use information, organize it and use different sources.

7b I can look at the design and suggest other ways.

7c I can produce a design proposal recording and explaining my decisions.

Planning and Making

3a I realize that some of the ideas I have may not be possible because I do not have enough time or the right sort of material.

3b I know enough about materials so that I can choose the right one for my activity.

3c I can use a range of hand tools correctly and safely.

3d I try out other ideas when my first idea doesn't work well.

4a I make sure that I don't waste any materials or use more than I need as it will be too expensive. I can work accurately.

4b I can work with others to plan an activity.

4c I can choose the right sorts of equipment and techniques for my activity.

4d I can change my plan when I find I am in difficulties, and know when to ask for help.

4e I can use drawings, diagrams and models to help me work out when I am going to do.

5a I can plan an activity well taking into account the best use of time and materials.

5b I know about a whole range of materials and can choose the best one for a particular job.

5c I can use a range of equipment safely and well, and known what should be used for each task.

5d I can overcome problems as they happen.

6a I can plan and organize an activity well.

6b I know the properties of a range of materials, and can choose those which are most sensible for my project.

6c I can see the limitations in a range of tools.

6d I can overcome obstacles.

6e I can seek advice and information once I have carefully thought about the idea myself.

6f I can use drawings, sketches, diagrams and plans to help me with my activity.

7a I can plan and complete an activity taking into account time limits, availability of materials, equipment and costs.

7b I can competently make use of a wide range of skills when undertaking an activity.

7c I can use drawings, sketches, diagrams and plans to help me plan and carry out an activity.

Evaluating

3a I can talk about what I have done, and say how well it may help other people.

3b I can talk about why I used certain materials and equipment and how well I carried out the task.

4a I can explain how and why my idea changed as I went through the activity.

4b At the end of an activity I can explain why I chose to use certain equipment and materials.

4c I can talk about things and places from here and from other times and places.

4d I can explain how technology has changed the way we live and effects the amount of money we can spend.

5a I can look at what I set out to do, and evaluate how well my product achieved this.

5b I can say why I chose to use the materials, equipment, techniques and processes that I did and say where I could have made improvements.

5c I can take into account the features of artefacts, systems and environments from other periods in history and from other cultures, and use this information in my own activities.

6a After trying my ideas I can decide whether it was worthwhile or whether I should have taken a different approach.

6b I can carry out tests to see if the outcome I have produced does do what I intended it to do.

6c I can look at the materials I have used and decide if they were the best ones to use.

6d I can look at the things I did and the way I did them and decide what could have been improved.

6e I can explain the effects which technology has had in the past and will have in the future in countries throughout the world, particularly with respect to the environment, money, society and money, and can give particular examples.

7a I can present an evaluation of an activity, saying how well it matched the original need and taking into account the views of people who have made use of it. I can use this evaluation in order to suggest improvements.

GLOSSARY

Artefact: something made by people, such as a poster, a piece of clothing, a chair.

Brainstorming: a way of thinking up ideas in a group, to come up with design ideas.

Campaign: an organised way of doing something.

Commercial product: something which is made to be sold.

Community: a place where people live and work.

Component: a part of a whole product which is separately designed and made.

Constraints: the factors which affect design such as cost, time and the equipment and materials that are available.

Context: the type of situation in which you can design and make something, for example, you can make a meal in the context of your home, school or restaurant.

Criteria: the means by which designs are judged and evaluated.

Database: a collection of information stored on a computer.

Design brief: a statement of what is needed in a design.

Design features: the parts which make up a design.

Environment: your surroundings – a park, buildings, rooms, streets.

Equipment: the tools and machinery which are used for making.

Evaluate: a way of finding out how effective and successful a design is.

Graphic designer: someone who designs visual products such as advertisements, book covers and lay-outs, labels and packaging.

Logo: a symbol for a product or organisation which shows their identity or image.

Materials: that which is used to make objects, for example paper, glue, food, paint, clay, wood, fabric, plastic . . .

Mechanism: part of a system of parts that work together to produce movement.

Model: a version of a design made in cheap materials or a smaller size so as to develop and test a design idea or show it to other people.

Pattern: a way of drawing up designs on materials before cutting them out.

Preference sampling: asking a **sample** of people what they prefer, for example, what holidays they prefer, what soft drink they like best . . .

Presentation drawing: realistic drawing giving a good idea of what the design will look like when its finished.

Presentation model: complete, realistic model of a design to show what the finished product will be like.

Product image: way of presenting products, or a company to make them appealing and interesting.

Prototype: an accurate model of a design, which can be tested.

Questionnaire: an ordered set of questions designed to give information about a topic or product.

Sample: a group of people selected for a survey, who are likely to have similar preferences or views to many others.

Scale drawing: drawing which is reduced or enlarged in exact proportion to the actual size of the design.

Survey: a way of finding things out by asking questions.

System: a set of activities or objects which carry out a task, for example a canteen or a stereo.

Target group: the group that the design product is for.

Testing panel: a group of people used to test different products, for example, shampoo, food or drink, to see which they like best.

Trial run: a test run to see if the design works and meets the designer's criteria for a good design.

Working drawing: detailed drawing that contains enough information for the design to be made.